Maggie Sansone

A Celtic Fair

Celtic & Renaissance Tunes for Hammered Dulcimer

Hammered dulcimer arrangements from advanced beginner to advanced levels transcribed from the recording *A Celtic Fair*. Chords included.

Edited by Paul Oorts

Online Audio   www.melbay.com/21734BCDEB

Audio Contents

1. Scottish Bransle
2. Celtic Jigs
3. Breton An Dro
4. Circle Dance
5. Dancing Reels
6. The Butterfly Slip Jig Set
7. Variations on Pretty Girl Milking a Cow
8. Highland Boat Song
9. Round of Loudéac/The Wren
10. Irish Reels
11. Maiden Lane
12. French Renaissance Dances

1 2 3 4 5 6 7 8 9 0

© 2009 MAGGIE'S MUSIC, INC. ALL RIGHTS RESERVED, USED BY PERMISSION.
WORLDWIDE DISTRIBUTION LICENSE BY MEL BAY PUBLICATIONS, INC. PACIFIC, MO 63069. MADE AND PRINTED IN U.S.A.
No part of this publication may be reproduced in whole or in part, or stored in a retrieval system, or transmitted in any form
or by any means, electronic, mechanical, photocopy, recording, or otherwise, without written permission of the publisher.

Visit us on the Web at www.melbay.com — E-mail us at email@melbay.com

Table of Contents

HOW TO USE THIS BOOK, EMBELLISHMENTS,
 ABOUT THE HAMMERED DULCIMER 3
ABOUT MAGGIE SANSONE,
 SELECTED DISCOGRAPHY 4
ABOUT THE RECORDING
 (FROM THE LINER NOTES) 5
REVIEWS FOR A CELTIC FAIR 6

THE TUNES:
(tunes are presented in the same order as they appear on the recording *A Celtic Fair*)
1. SCOTTISH BRANSLE, Intro 8
2. SCOTTISH BRANSLE,
 Gm and Am, melody and chords 9
3. SCOTTISH BRANSLE, Gm, in 4 parts 10
4. SCOTTISH BRANSLE, Am, in 4 parts 12
5. BRETON JIG, melody and chords 14
6. BRETON JIG, arrangement 15
7. CASTLEBAR, melody and chords 16
8. CASTLEBAR, arrangement 17
9. TRAIN TO DUBLIN, melody and chords 18
10. TRAIN TO DULBIN, arrangement 19
11. BRETON AN DRO, F#m- 1st round 20
12. BRETON AN DRO, Bm- 2nd and 3rd round 21
13. CIRCLE DANCE, melody and chords 22
14. CIRCLE DANCE, arrangement 23
15. WATCHMAKER, melody and chords
 in 2 octaves 24
16. WATCHMAKER, arrangement 25
17. HIGH REEL, melody and chords 26
18. SILVER SPEAR, melody and chords 27
19. COMB YOUR HAIR AND CURL IT,
 melody and chords 28
20. COMB YOUR HAIR AND CURL IT,
 arrangement 29
21. BUTTERFLY, melody and chords 30
22. BUTTERFLY, arrangement 31
23. BARNEY BRALLAGHAN, melody and chords .. 32
24. BARNEY BRALLAGHAN, arrangement 33
25. VARIATION on PRETTY GIRL MIKLING A COW,
 melody and chords 34
26. VARIATION on PRETTY GIRL MILKING A COW,
 3 page arrangement 35
27. HIGHLAND BOAT SONG,
 arrangement with alternate chords 39
28. HIGHLAND BOAT SONG,
 2 page arrangement with variation 40
29. ROUND OF LOUDEAC,
 melody and chords in 2 octaves 43
30. ROUND OF LOUDEAC, 2 page arrangement 44
31. THE WREN, melody and chords 47
32. THE WREN, 2 page arrangement 48
33. DONEGAL HIGHLAND,
 melody and back up arrangement 50
34. DONEGAL HIGHLAND, arrangement 51
35. MOTHER AND CHILD, melody and chords 52
36. WOMAN OF THE HOUSE, melody and chords 53
37. MAIDEN LANE, G and A, melody and chords .. 54
38. FRENCH RENAISSANCE DANCES,
 melody and chords 56
39. FRENCH RENAISSANCE DANCES,
 2-part arrangements 57

INDEX, tunes in alphabetical order 58

Acknowledgments

Many thanks to Paul Oorts, Ken Kolodner.
my producer Bobby Read and all the musicians who shared their talents
and creativity in the making of the recording *A Celtic Fair*.
Credits:
At the Celtic Fair, R.Crenshaw,
Carcassonne, Galen Frysinger,
HammerHands, Barbara Silcox.
Artist photo, Fred Shively.
Audio cover design, Amy White

www.maggiesmusic.com

Maggie's Music

How to Use this Book

Most hammered dulcimer players today own 14/15 dulcimers, or larger instruments with extended ranges and more chromatic notes, but all the tunes and arrangements in this book fit easily on smaller dulcimers as well. The recording A Celtic Fair includes much musical variety and complexity in their arrangements with the hammered dulcimer often in ensemble arrangements with other instruments. This makes it hard to hear the dulcimer at times and for this music book, I have included a variety of transcriptions of the basic melody and also created new arrangements for different levels of playing from beginning to advanced. Chords are provided to identify the harmonic structure of the tune and give the opportunity to explore other arrangement ideas on your own. Listening to the recording will enrich the musician's understanding and spirit of the melody.

Embellishments

Much of the beauty of hammered dulcimer music comes from the instrument's wide range of idiomatic embellishments. This collection notates those embellishments as they appear throughout the book and below are more detailed explanations.

Flam. A Flam is indicated by the two small bared eighth notes preceding the main note. (the first small note is always higher in tone than the second note, which is played on the bass bridge). The flam is a technique used to produce 3 notes as follows: The right hammer will play two notes by allowing the right hammer to hit the first note and bounce across the string at an angle to the bass bridge and hit the second note while the left hammer strikes the main note.

Grace Note – A grace note is shown as a small note directly preceding a primary note.

Roll – A roll is a technique used to play a chord of three or more notes. Play the notes from the bottom up.

Bounded Triplet or bounced double note: This is 2 or 3 notes played with just one hammer stroke; indicated by 2 or 3 small notes proceeding the primary note. Sometimes a hammering suggestion is indicated: R * which means: play the first note with the Right hammer and let it bounce 1 time to sound the second note. R ** means let the hammer bounce 2 more times.

About the Hammered Dulcimer

The hammered dulcimer is a trapezoid-shaped wooden box with over seventy-five metal strings stretched across its top and played with wooden mallets. The ancestor of the piano, it originated in ancient Persia and was introduced to Europe by the returning crusaders and played throughout the medieval and renaissance times. Since its introduction by British settlers to the American shores, the dulcimer has increased in popularity and is well suited in many genres of music including Appalachian, bluegrass, Celtic and world music. Its popularity continues to grow as more enthusiasts discover this unique and versatile instrument.

About Maggie Sansone

America's premier hammered dulcimer player, Maggie Sansone brings a special beauty and vision to her music. Praised as "one of the most exciting and innovative hammered dulcimer players records today, with a fire and passion to her playing" by Dirty Linen Folk & World, Sansone's pioneering artistry has brought the resonant beauty of the hammered dulcimer to thousands of music lovers around the world. Born in Miami, Florida, Maggie has played music all her life, from piano and guitar to banjo and the bassoon. She received a BFA in Fine Arts from Kent State University, Kent, Ohio, and after travels through Europe, Egypt and Turkey moved to Maryland in the mid-70's where she established Maggie's Music first as folk music studio then a record label. After discovering the hammered dulcimer in 1980, she decided to make it her principal instrument. Her music has been hailed as a fusion of ancient sounds and modern sensibility, fueled by the innovative integration of old and new instruments. Sansone has been featured on CBS-TV Sunday Morning, and NPR's All Things Considered, Performance Today and Fiona Ritchie's The Thistle & Shamrock. She has also won numerous awards including the ANNIE award for Performing Arts (Anne Arundel Country Cultural Arts Foundation, Maryland), the WAMMIE award Celtic Instrumentalist (Washington Area Music Association, Washington D.C.) and INDIE awards for her recordings. Active as a concert producer and performer in Celtic and Christmas shows, Sansone tours throughout the United States, performing at a variety of venues from folk and Celtic festivals to the America's Kennedy Center. In addition to her performing career, Sansone is the author of a series of hammered dulcimer music books published by Mel Bay Publications. Mel Bay included her in their Hammered dulcimer Anthology Series featuring America's finest performers and teachers. Sansone is the founder and CEO of the Maggie's Music record label. Founded in 1984, the label features twelve recording artists and over fifty recordings distributed worldwide, including her solo recordings. Maggie's Music has received eight "Record Label of the Year" WAMMIE awards and praise from Fiona Ritchie (NPR's The Thistle & Shamrock) who said, "Maggie's Music is a gathering place of much Celtic rooted and inspired acoustic music in the USA."

Selected Discography
A Celtic Fair (MM112)
Merrily Greet the Time (MM228) with Sue Richards
Celtic Meditations: Into the Light (MM302)
Mystic Dance: A Celtic Celebration (MM 111)
A Traveler's Dream (MM110)
Dance Upon the Shore (MM109)
Ancient Noels (MM108) with Ensemble Galilei
A Scottish Christmas (MM215) with Bonnie Rideout and Al Petteway
Music in the Great Hall (MM107) with Ensemble Galilei
Mist and Stone (MM106)
Sounds of the Season II (MM105)
Sounds of the Season (MM103)
Traditions (MM104)

About the Recording

(excerpts from the liner notes)

A Celtic Fair (Maggie's Music, MM112)
Come to the Celtic fair for a festive gathering of tradition and innovation, Celtic music, a Renaissance spirit, diverse instrumentation and arrangements and spellbinding percussive grooves. Performed on hammered dulcimer, Irish flute, fiddle, soprano sax, woodwinds, guitar, accordion, smallpipes, bodhran and percussion. "In choosing this music, I was inspired by all of my musical experiences—from performing on large concert stages to joining in on Irish sessions at neighborhood pubs; playing a wedding processional march, and jigs for a children's maypole; offering an elegant pavane to King Henry VIII at a Renaissance festival and accompanying a set of reels for Irish step dancers at a Celtic fair. Come join us now for a festive gathering at the Celtic fair!" –Maggie Sansone

1. Scottish Bransle (pronounced "brawl") An improvisation in a minor mode serves as an intro to this mysterious Renaissance dance published in *Orchesographie* (1589) by dance master Thoinot Arbeau (1520-1595).

2. Celtic Jigs. Picture a musical journey starting on the rocky Brittany coast with the *Breton Jig*, traveling across the sea to Ireland with a stop at *Castlebar*, in the western part of Ireland, where you hop on a *Train to Dublin* (©Maggie Sansone) a 150-mile ride that will complete our journey!

3. Breton An Dro. An Dro (Breton: "the turn") is an open circle dance in 2/4 with dancers linking their pinky fingers. Brittany, one of the six Celtic nations is located on the northwest coast of France and still retains its Celtic culture and language to this day. Imagine a gathering of musicians in colorful garb, instruments in hand, heading for merriment and revelry at the castle fair.

4. Circle Dance. A traditional Breton tune called an An Dro, where the dancers link their pinky fingers and go around together in a circle. The melody is based on an ancient modal scale and its repeating phrases has a mesmerizing sound that draws the listener into the world of the ancient Celts.

5. Dancing Reels (*The Watchmaker/Highland Reel/Silver Spear*). These are well-traveled tunes heard in Northumberland, Ireland, Scotland and America.

6. The Butterfly Set includes slip jigs in 9/8: *Comb Your Hair and Curl It, The Butterfly,* an Irish step dancing favorite that lends itself to jazzy rhythms; and *Barney Brallaghan*.

7. Variations on Pretty Girl Milking a Cow. Solo hammered dulcimer. This Irish air begins with the melancholy refrain and adds new variations throughout, ending in an upbeat mood.

8. Highland Boat Song. A beautiful air from Scotland also known as *The Arran Boat Song*.

9. Round de Loudeac/The Wren. A set of traditional Breton tunes.

10. Irish Reels. This set starts with *Donegal Highland*, played as a slow air that picks up tempo into two Irish session tunes, *Mother and Child* and *Woman of the House*.

11. Maiden Lane. An English country dance tune that has become the "hit tune" at the Maryland Renaissance Festival where it is played for King Henry and his court.

12. French Renaissance Dances (Première Suytte de Branles d'Ecosse). Four 16th century Renaissance dance tunes called branles (pronounced "brawl") from The Attaingnant Dance Prints (1557) published by Pierre Attaingnant (ca.1529-ca.1557).

Here's what they're saying...

"Sansone opens the perception of Celtic music far beyond the usual sources with A Celtic/New Age/jazzy sound that bubbles with life ." Rock 'N' Reel Magazine (U.K)

"A virtuoso with a world-class gift as both a player and arranger, Sansone interprets the folk idiom on an ancient instrument with a modern voice and presents the listener with a unique opportunity for mystery and mysticism." Women Today

"Harmoniously walking the tightrope between ancient Celtic cadences and progressive world beat sounds, Sansone easily fuses the best of past and present musical styles" New Age Retailer

"A visionary meeting of Celtic and world music influences, Sansone explores the entire palette of dulcimer sounds, alternately expressing its melodic, percussive and harmonic sides." AFIM (Association for Independent Music)

"Steeped in tradition yet often wed to the contemporary...with unexpected color, rhythmic vitality and a venturesome spirit." The Washington Post

"The most exciting and innovative hammered dulcimer player recording today...She has a fire and passion to her playing!" Dirty Linen Folk & World Music Magazine

"In Sansone's hands, the hammered dulcimer not only dances, it swings. With understanding and musicianship, she adapts traditional tunes suited to it while retaining their Celtic roots." Irish Edition

REVIEWS for *A Celtic Fair*
"Maggie Sansone has created a niche for herself playing Celtic music on the hammered dulcimer. There's real substance to the music, a true love of the genre, and plenty of research to complement the musicianship." All Music Guide (AMG)

"The ancient hammered dulcimer, according to Maggie Sansone, has "followed the migrations of early travelers across Asia Minor to the European continent." And in these 12 pieces, Sansone and company have pushed that versatile instrument on into the 21st century. This collection rings with the rich melodies of centuries-old compositions, presented in ways their original composers could never have imagined. The arrangements include not only the typical Celtic mix- Irish flute, fiddle, bodhrán -but the addition of such instruments as woodwinds and even sax that lend a contemporary, even jazz-new-age flavor, creating pensive tones, mystical auras and all manner of merriment. Sansone performs masterfully on hammered dulcimer and smallpipes, along with Sara Read on fiddle and Rob Greenway (guitar, Irish flute, button accordion). Most notable, however, is the contribution of Bobby Read as producer and performer on sax, clarinet, bass clarinet, flutes, accordion, woodwinds, keyboards, percussion and drum programming). He also performs with the Bruce Hornsby Band. Read's innovative arrangements and seamless engineering allow the material to retain its Celtic sensibility, which is only enhanced by the some brilliant innovation. Standout tracks include "Breton An Dro," in which delicate string-reedy tones are overtaken by the silky, gentle swing of a sax. In this richly textured presentation, the artists demonstrate just how much can be accomplished within a simple, repetitive melody. There are two jig sets, the typical toe-tapper "Breton Jig/Castlebar/Train to Dublin" (Sansone's original) and the more moody "Comb Your Hair & Curl It/The Butterfly/Barney Brallaghan." The lovely "Variations on an Irish Air (Pretty Girl Milking the Cow)" has all the emotional impact of the most heart-wrenching traditional song. Throughout, Sansone performs in that hold-your-breath emotive style that has the listener hanging onto every note, and for sure it will be a delight." Dirty Linen Folk & World Magazine

1. Scottish Bransle, intro

Scottish Bransle published in *Orchesographie* (1589) by Thoinot Arbeau (1520-1595

(c) 2009, Maggie Sansone

From the CD: A Celtic Fair

Based on ancient modes, this introduction was inspired by the mysterious qualities of the bransle which follows.

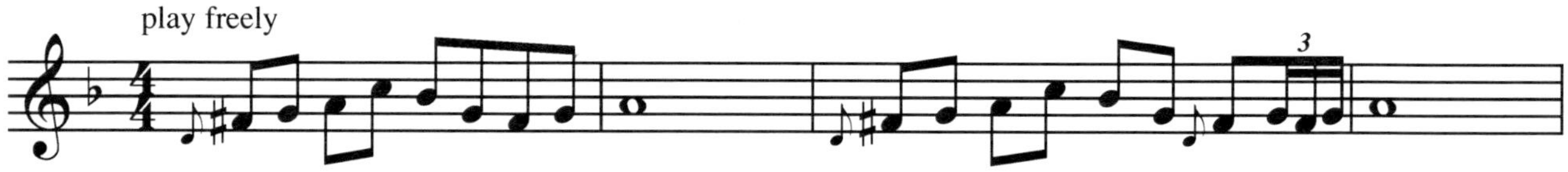

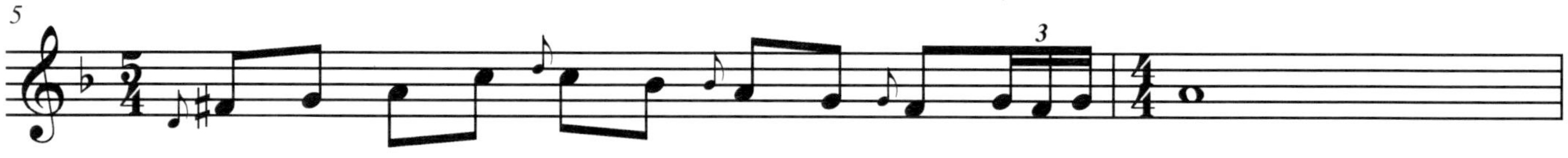

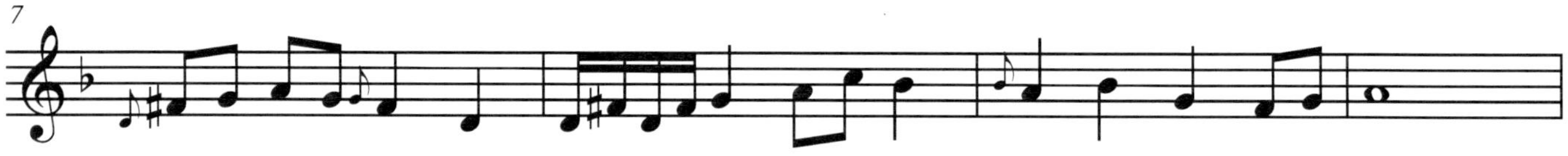

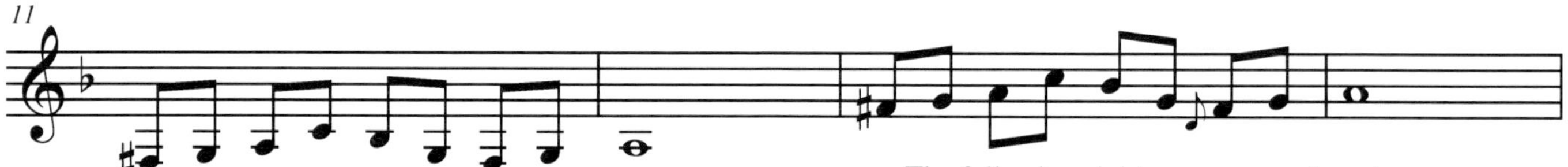

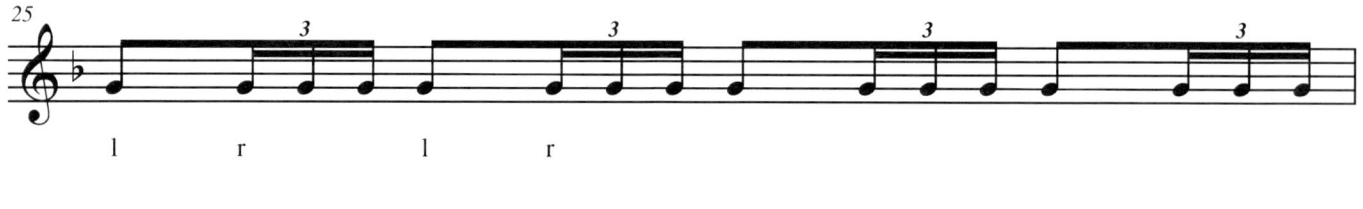

The following eight measures are based on the Arabic scale at the bottom of this page.

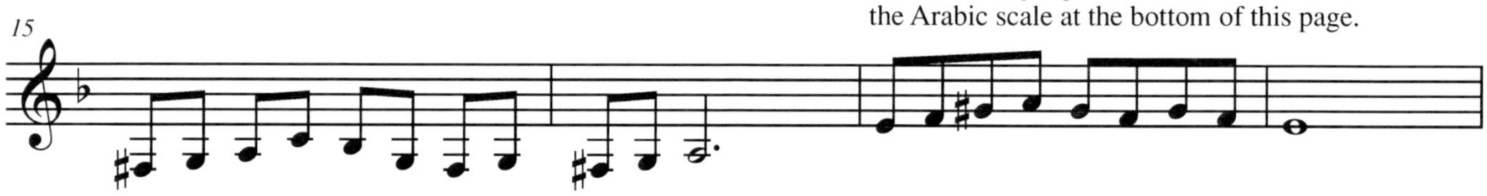

Tremolo- marked with slash marks over stem is played with rapid **r** (right) and **l** (left) hammerd strikes on one string.

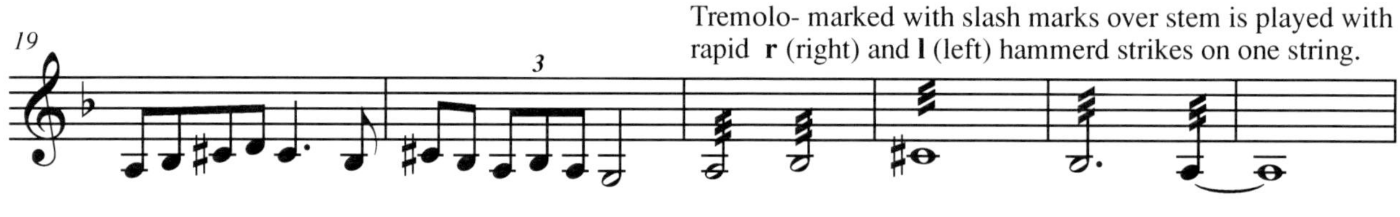

This rhythm leads into the melody of the Scottish bransle (2.)
It uses the bounced triplet that is played by letting your hammer bounce on one string 2 -3 times.

26 Arabic scale

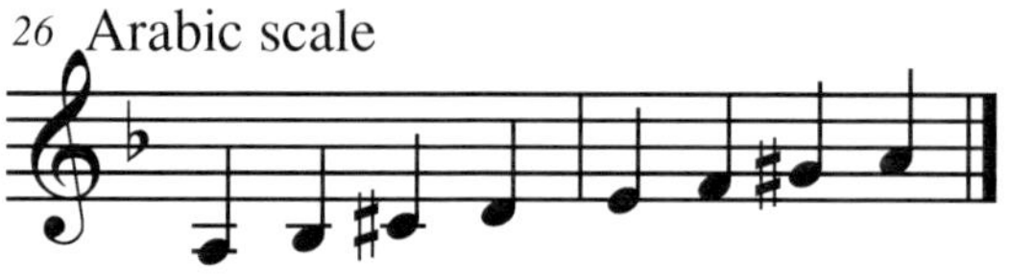

2. Scottish Bransle

Key of Gm and Am
melody and chords

From Orchesographie (1589)
published by Thoinot Arbeau (1520-1595)
Arr. Maggie Sansone
(c) 2009, Maggies' Music
From the CD: A Celtic Fair

3. Scottish Bransle, in four parts

Key of Gm

From *Orchesography* (1589)
by Thoinot Arbeau (1520-1595)
Arr. Maggie Sansone
(c) 2009, Maggie' sMusic
From CD: A Celtic Fair

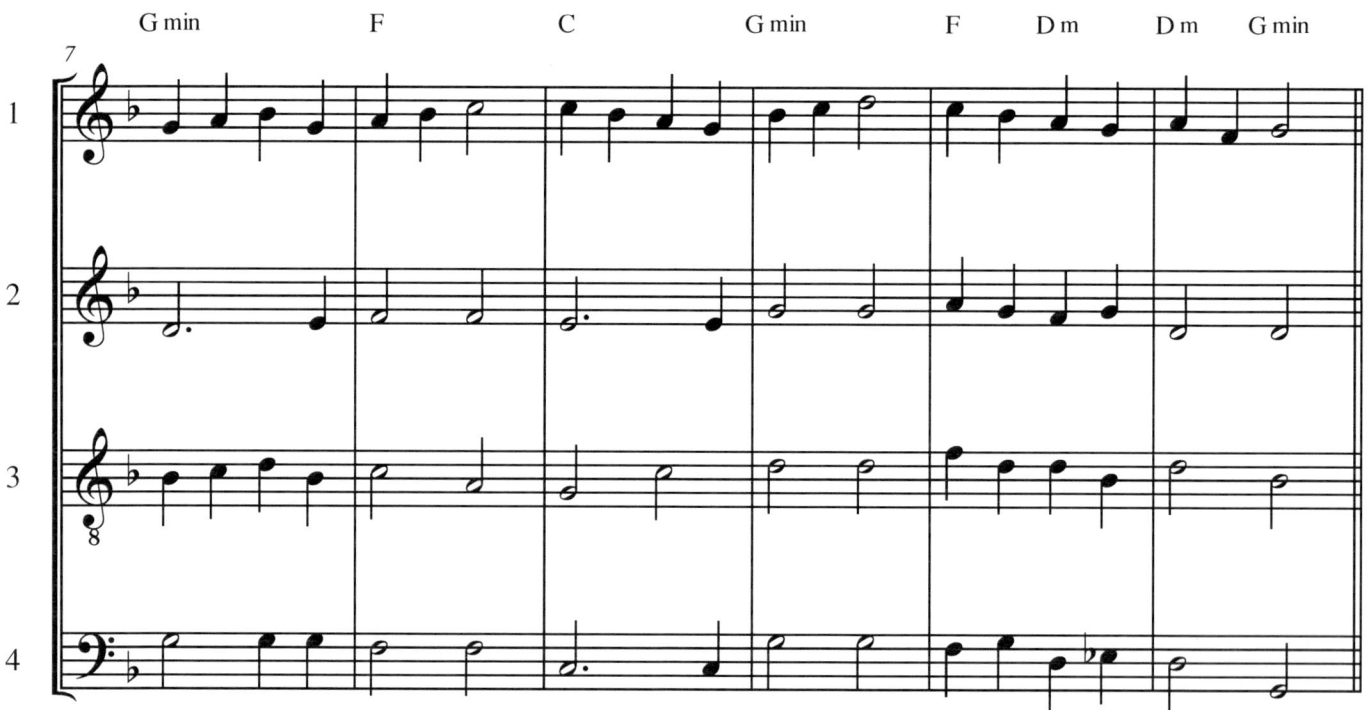

page 2--Scottish Bransle, Gm arrangement in 4 Parts

11

4. Scottish Bransle, in four parts

Key of Am

From *Orchesographie* (1589) by
Thoinot Arbeau (1520-1595)
Arr. Maggie Sansone
(c) 2009, Maggie's Music
From the CD: A Celtic Fair

page 2--Scottish Bransle, Am arrangement in 4 parts

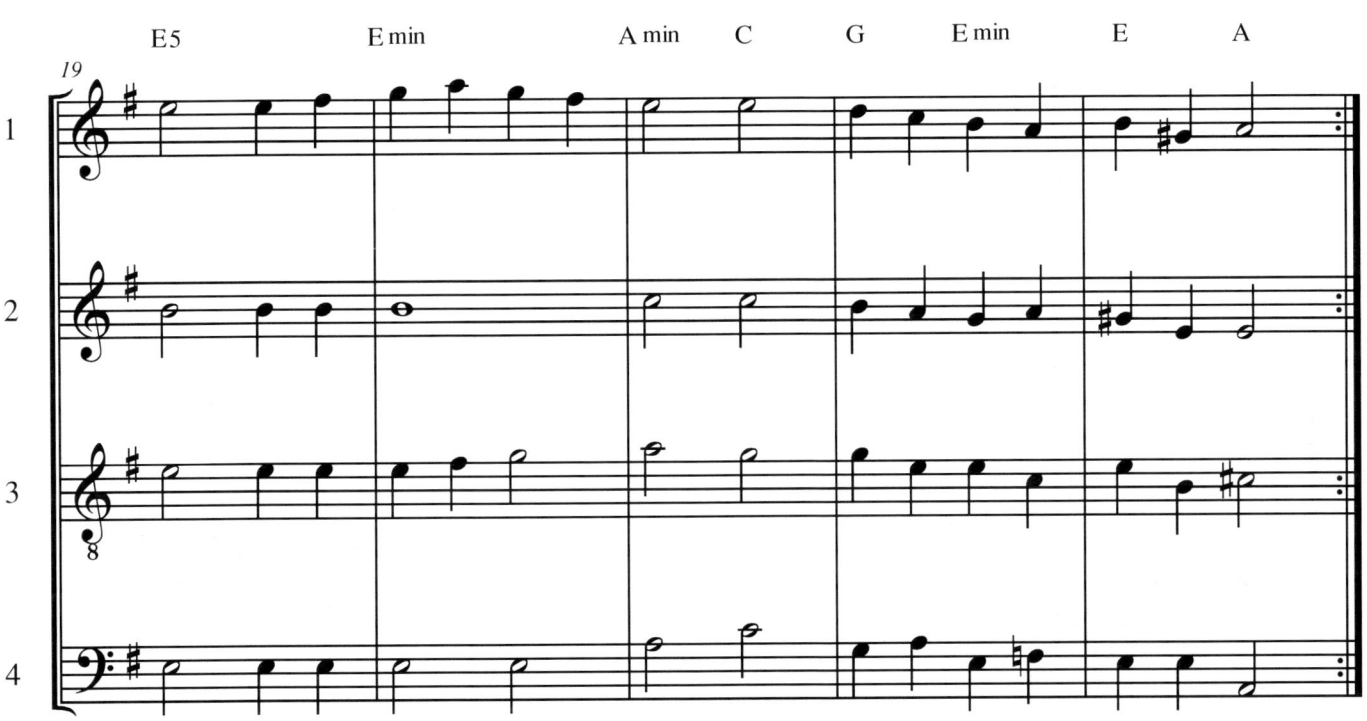

13

5. Breton Jig
melody and chords

Traditional Breton Tune
Arr. Maggie Sansone
(c) 2009 Maggie's Music
From the CD: A Celtic Fair

6. Breton Jig

Hammered Dulcimer Arrangement
with moving bass line, flams and bounced triplets

Traditional Breton tune
Arr. Maggie Sansone
(c) 2009, Maggie's Music
From the CD: A Celtic Fair

7. Castlebar

melody and chords

Traditional Irish Jig
Arr. Maggie Sansone
(c) 2009 Maggie's Music
From the CD: A Celtic Fair

8. Castlebar

Hammered Dulcimer Arrangement
This tune is played in 2 keys: A part: G major, B part: E dorian

Trational Irish Jig
Arr. Maggie Sansone
(c) 2009 Maggie's Music
From the CD: A Celtic Fair

R * * = another way of notating bounced triplets: **R** hammer hits first of the 3 notes, and then bounces to play the other **2** notes as indicated by *

9. Train to Dublin

melody and chords

(c) Maggie Sansone
(c) 2009, Maggie's Music
From the CD: A Celtic Fair

10. Train to Dublin

Hammered Dulcimer Arrangement

(c) Maggie Sansone
(c) 2009 Maggie's Music
From the CD: A Celtic Fair

* Bounced Triplet: R*=Right hammer strikes first note and bounces 1 more time to produce next note indicated by *.

__ = A dash under note means to play that note on the bass bridge

11. Breton An Dro in F#m

melody and chords

Traditional Breton tune
Arr. Maggie Sansone
(c) 2009, Maggie's Music
From the CD: A Celtic Fair

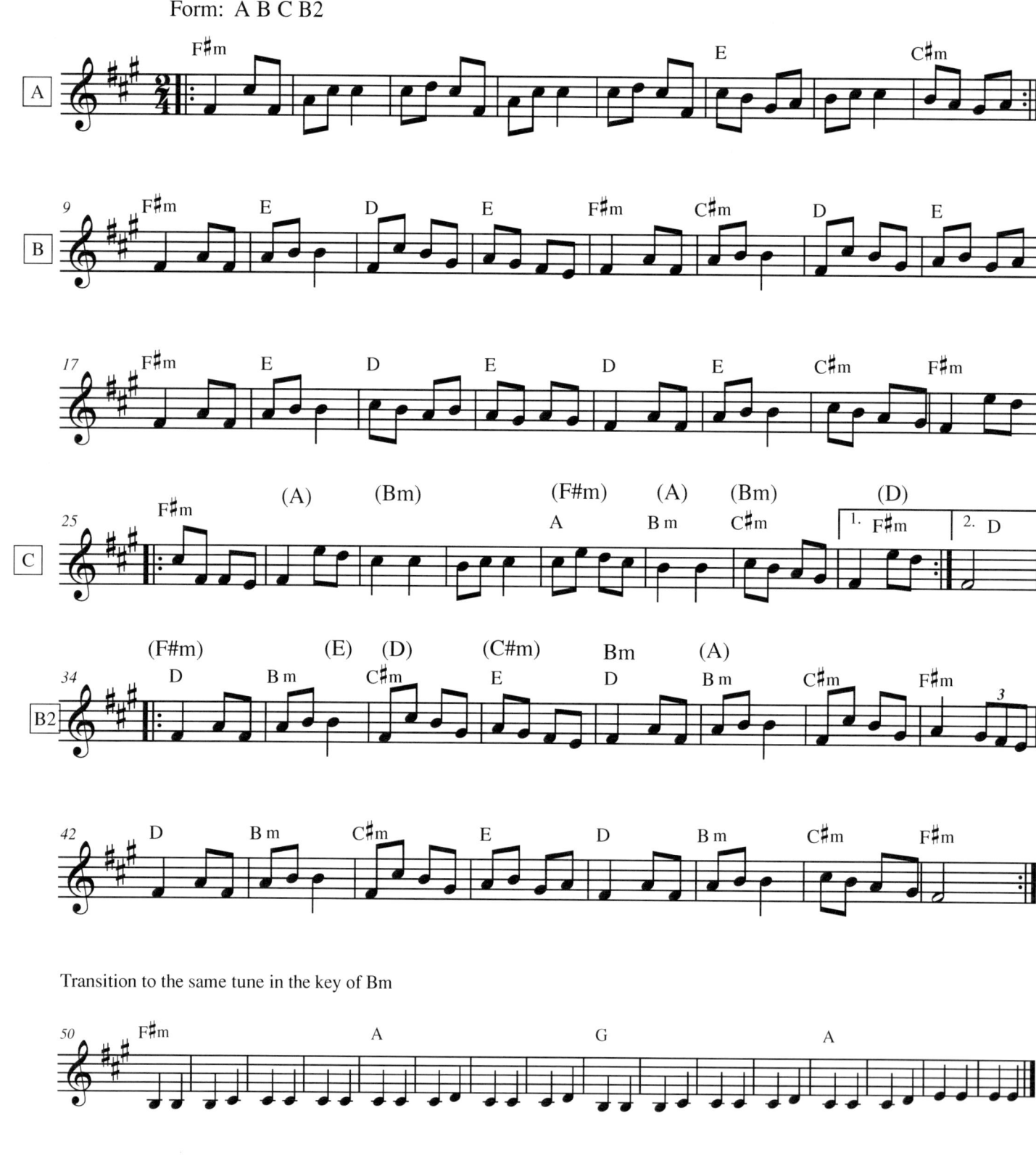

20

12. Breton An Dro in Bm

2nd and 3rd round

Traditional Breton tune
Arr. Maggie Sansone
(c) 2009 Maggie's Music
From the CD: A Celtic Fair

13. Circle Dance
melody and chords

Traditional Breton Tune
Arr. Maggie Sansone
(c) 2009 Maggie's Music
From the CD: A Celtic Fair

Form: AABB, AABB, AABB, Interlude, A

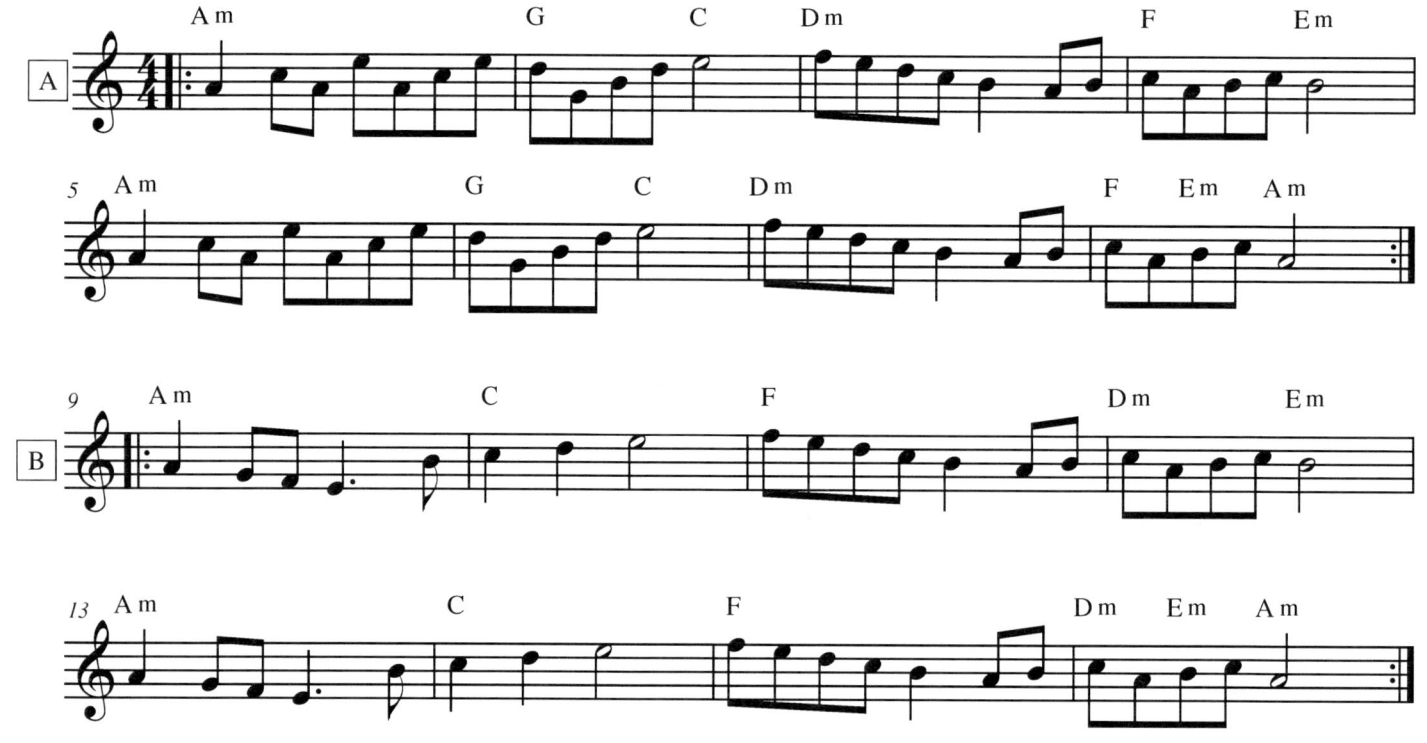

Interlude (Play freely improvising with this melody and Arabic Scale: A Bb C D E F G)

14. Circle Dance

Hammered Dulcimer Arrangement
with alternate chords and bass runs

Traditional Breton Tune
Arr. Maggie Sansone
(c) 2009 Maggie's Music
From the CD: A Celtic Fair

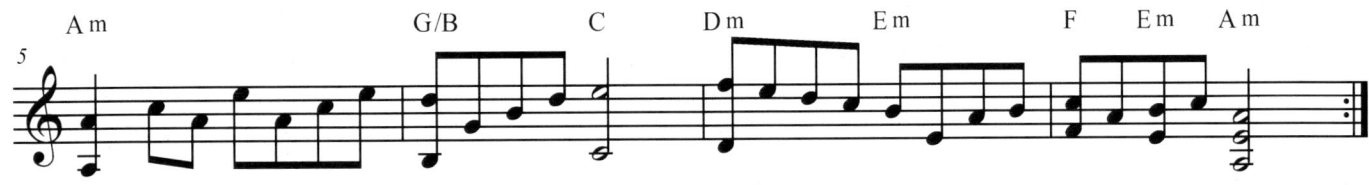

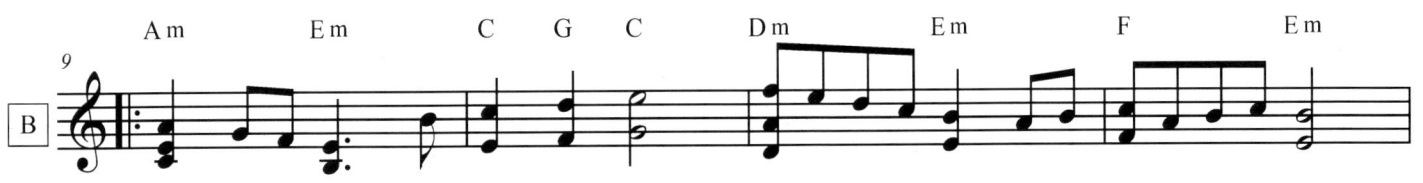

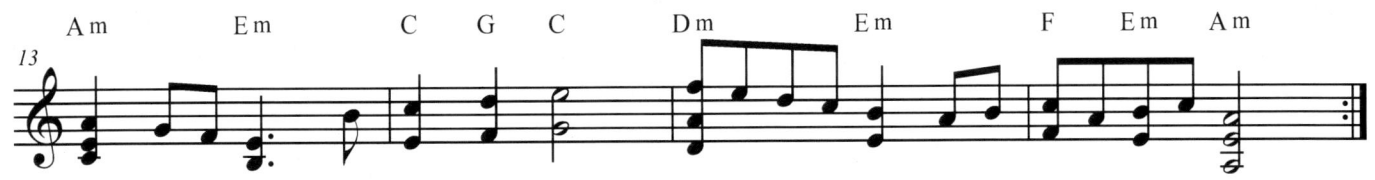

23

15. The Watchmaker

melody and chords in two octaves

Traditional Northumberland tune
Arr. Maggie Sansone
(c) 2009 Maggie's Music
From the CD: A Celtic Fair

16. The Watchmaker
Hammered Dulcimer Arrangement

Traditional Northumberland tune
Arr. Maggie Sansone
(c) 2009 Maggie's Music
From the CD: A Celtic Fair

Variation for mearuses 5 and 6:

17. High Reel

melody and chords

Traditional Scottish/Irish reel
Arr. Maggie Sansone
(c) 2009 Maggie's Music
From the CD: A Celtic Fair

L   LR LR L*R   L RLR ...

L R*

18. Silver Spear
Hammered Dulcimer Arrangement

Traditional Irish reel
Arr. Maggie Sansone
(c) 2009 Maggie's Music
From the CD: A Celtic Fair

19. Comb Your Hair and Curl It

melody and chords

Traditional Irish Slip Jig
Arr. Maggie Sansone
(c) 2009 Maggie's Music
From the CD: A Celtic Fair

20. Comb Your Hair and Curl It
Hammered Dulcimer Arrangement

Traditional Irish Slip Jig
Arr. Maggie Sansone
(c) 2009 Maggie's Music
From the CD: A Celtic Fair

21. The Butterfly
melody and chords

Traditional Irish Slip Jig
Arr. Maggie Sansone
(c) 2009 Maggie's Music
From the CD: A Celtic Fair

Variation for first three measures of the A section:

22. The Butterfly
Hammered Dulcimer Arrangement

Traditional Irish Slip Jig
Arr. Maggie Sansone
(c) 2009 Maggie's Music
From the CD: A Celtic Fair

Variation for the first three measures of the A section:

23. Barney Brallaghan

melody and chords

Traditional Irish Slip Jig
Arr. Maggie Sansone
(c) 2009 Maggie's Music
From the CD: A Celtic Fair

24. Barney Brallaghan
Hammered Dulcimer Arrangement

Traditional Irish Slip Jig
Arr. Maggie Sansone
(c) 2009 Maggie's Music
From the CD: A Celtic Fair

25. Variations on Pretty Girl Milking a Cow

melody and chords

Traditional Irish Air
Arr. Maggie Sansone
(c) 2009 Maggie's Music
From the CD: A Celtic Fair

26. Variations on Pretty Girl Milking a Cow

Hammered Dulcimer Arrangement

Traditional Irish Air
with original variations
Arr. Maggie Sansone
(c) 2009, Maggie's Music
From the CD: A Celtic Fair

FORM: A B C D E F E, final chord

page2--Variations on Pretty Girl Milking a Cow

page 3--Variations on Pretty Girl Milking a Cow

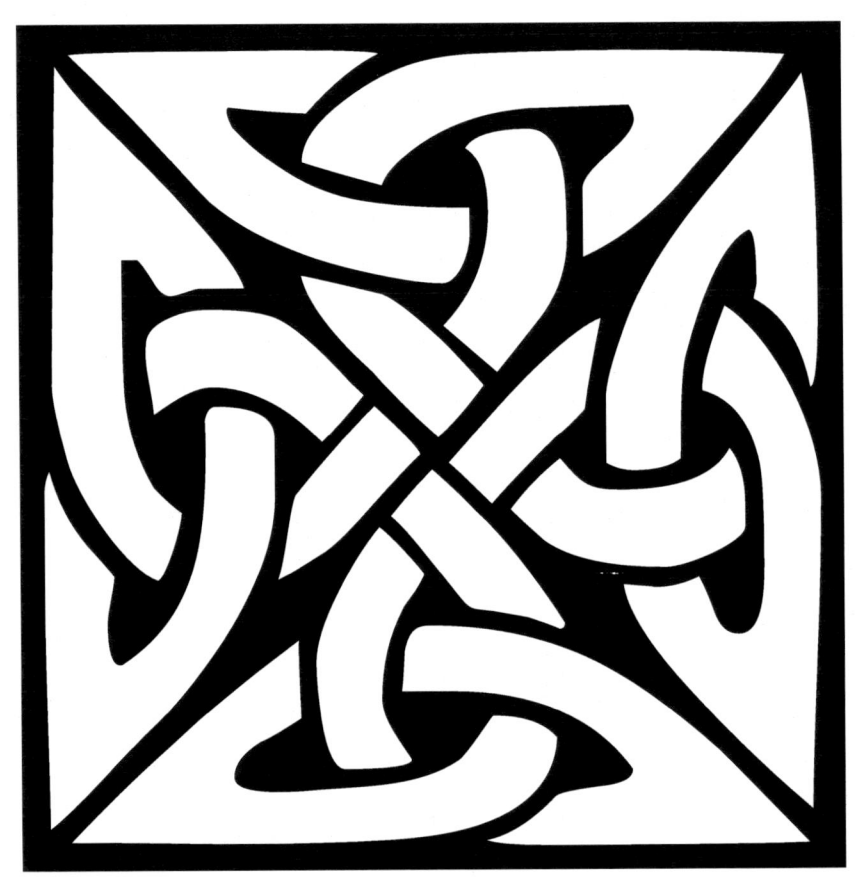

27. Highland Boat Song
Hammered Dulcimer Arrangement with alternate chords

Traditional Scottish air
Arr. Maggie Sansone
(c) 2009 Maggie's Music
From CD: A Celtic Fair

28. Highland Boat Song
Hammered Dulcimer Arrangement with Variation

Traditional Scottish air
Arr. Maggie Sansone with original variation. (c) 2009 Maggie's M
From the CD: A Celtic Fair

page 2--Highland Boat Song

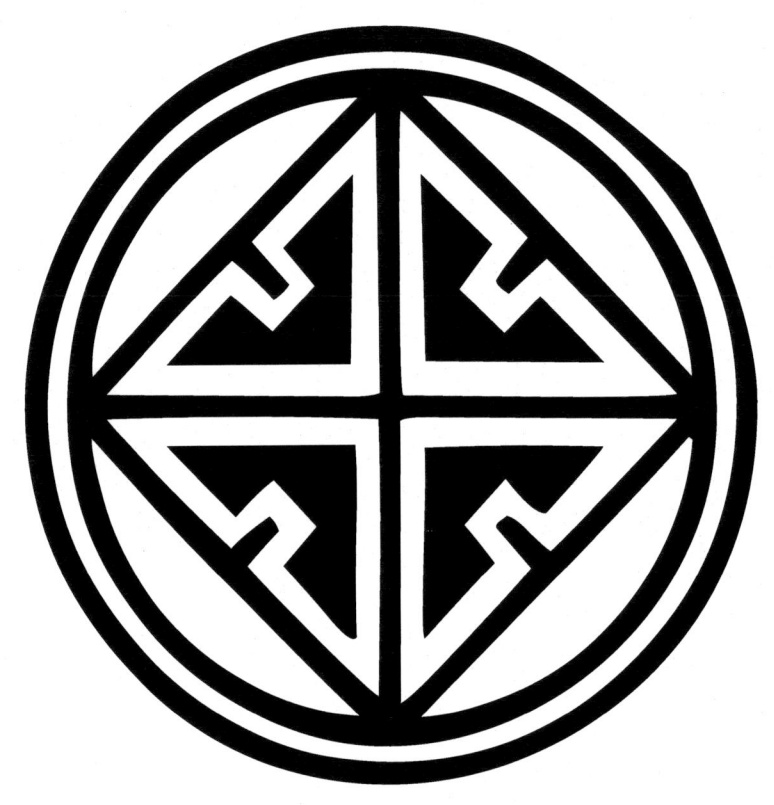

29. Round of Loudeac

Ronde de Loudéac
melody and chords in lower and upper octaves

Traditional Breton tune
Arr. Maggie Sansone
(c) 2009 Maggie's Music
From the CD: A Celtic Fair

30. Round of Loudeac

Ronde de Loudéac
Hammered Dulcimer two-page arrangement

Traditional Breton Tune
Arr. Maggie Sansone
(c) 2009 Maggie's Music
From the CD: A Celtic Fair

44

page 2-- Ronde de Loudac : variation in upper octave

31. The Wren

melody and chords

Traditional Breton Tune
Arr. Maggie Sansone
(c) 2009 Maggie's Music
From the CD: A Celtic Fair

32. The Wren

Hammered Dulcimer Arrangement, two pages

Traditional Breton Tune
Arr. Maggie Sansone
(c) 2009 Maggie's Music
From the CD: A Celtic Fair

page 2--The Wren

33. Donegal Highland

melody and chords, back up arrangement

Traditional Irish Reel
Arr. Maggie Sansone
(c) 2009 Maggie's Music
From the CD: A Celtic Fair

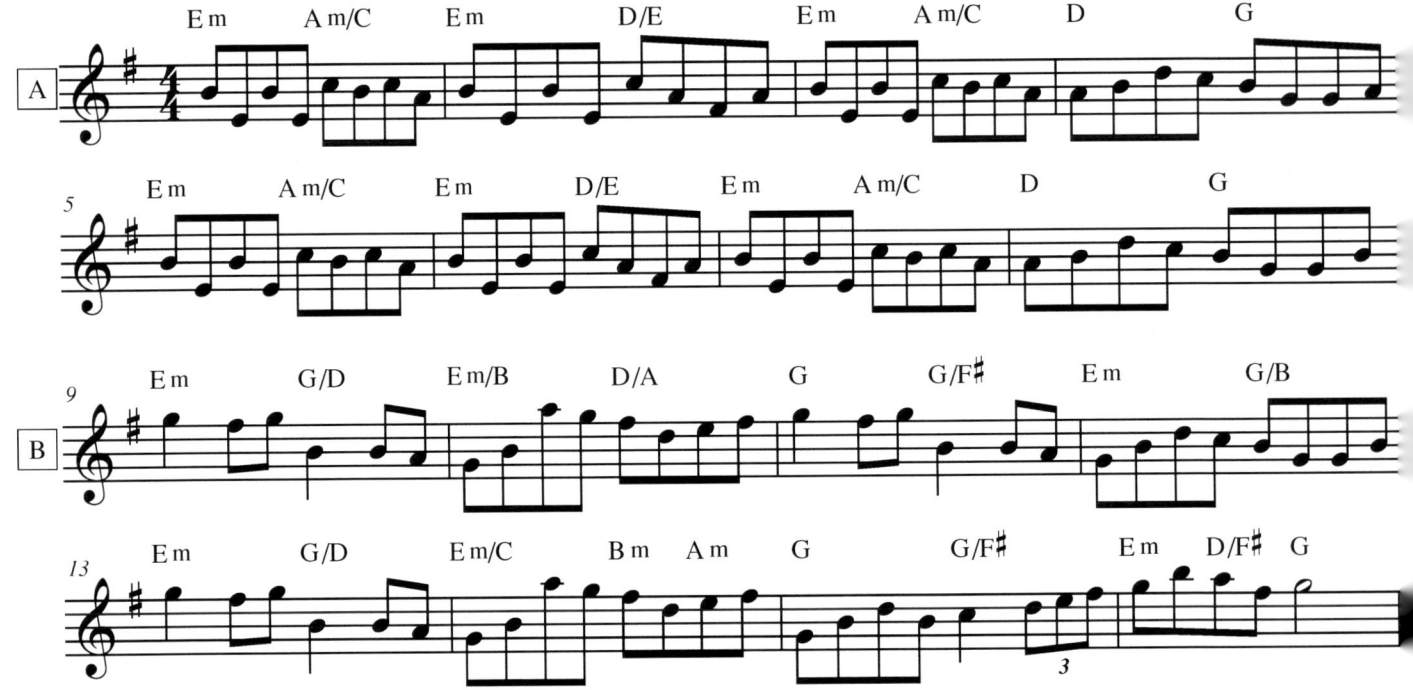

Donegal Highland: Backup

34. Donegal Highland
Hammered Dulcimer Arrangement

Traditional Irish reel,
played as a slow air
Arr. Maggie Sansone
(c) 2009 Maggie's Music
From the CD: A Celtic Fair

35. Mother and Child Basic

melody and chords

Traditional Irish reel
Arr. Maggie Sansone
(c) 2009 Maggie's Music
From the CD: A Celtic Fa

Form: A B, (each section is 8 measures long).

Last time through tune, play alternative chords in section B:

36. Woman of the House
melody and chords

Traditional Irish Reel
Arr. Maggie Sansone
(c) 2009 Maggie's Music
From the CD: A Celtic Fair

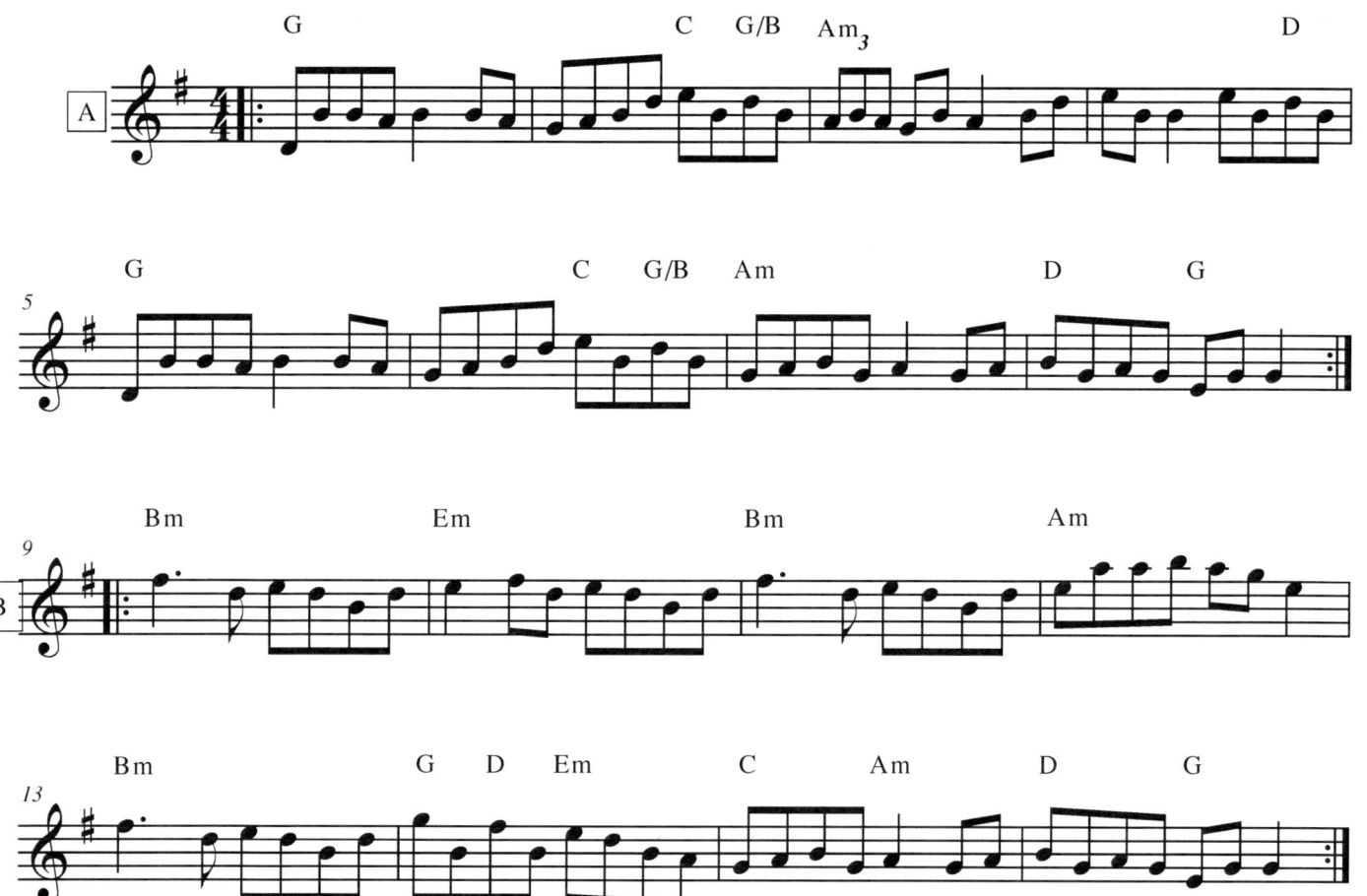

37. Maiden Lane

Key of G and A

John Playford
The Dancing Master, 1651
Arr. Maggie Sansone
(c) 2009 Maggie's Music
From the CD: A Celtic Fai[r]

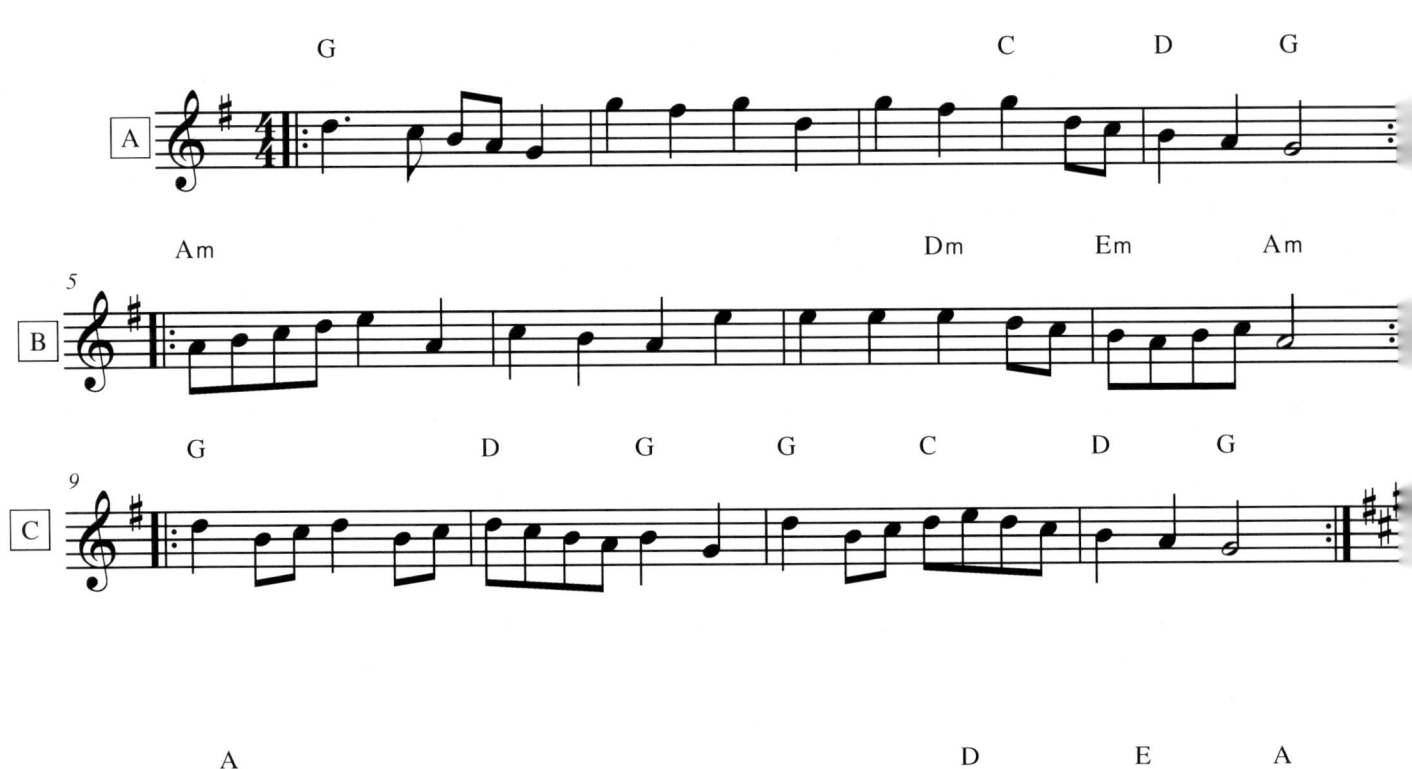
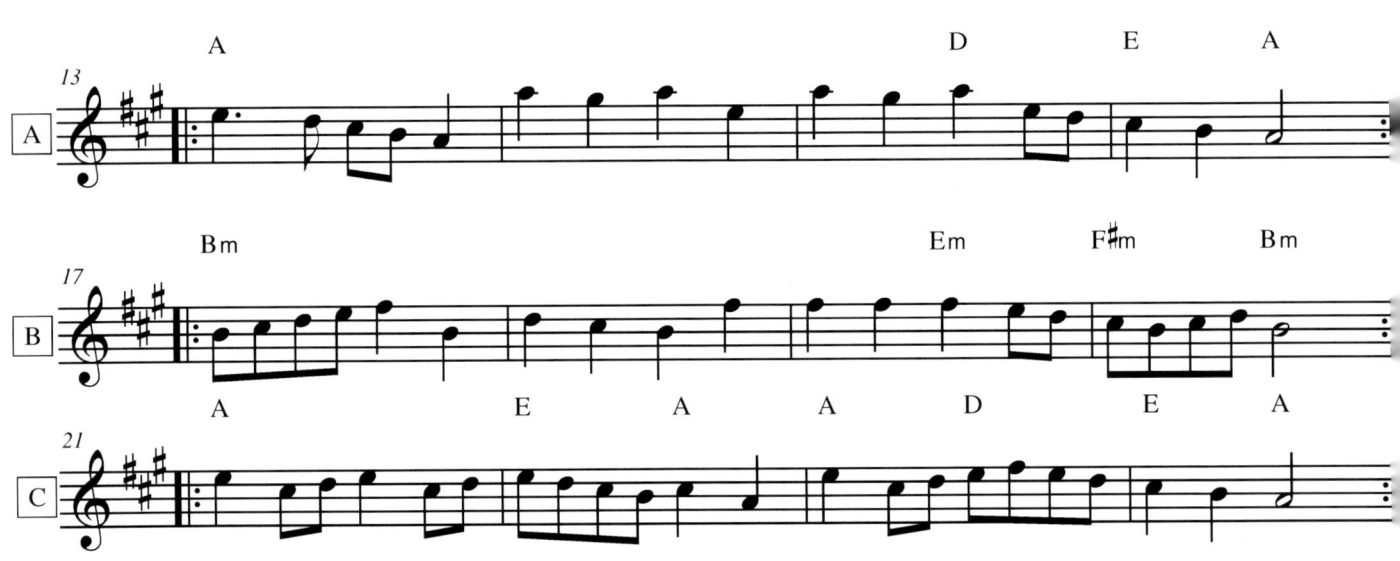

38. French Renaissance Dances

Premiere Suytte de Bransles d'Escosse
melody and chords

Pierre Attaingnant (ca.1529-1557)
The Attaingnant Dance Prints (1557)
Arr. Maggie Sansone
(c) 2009 Maggie's Music
From the CD: A Celtic Fair

39. French Renaissance Dances

Premiere Suytte de Bransles d'Escosse
Three dances arranged as duos for two melody instruments by Paul Oorts

Pierre Attaingnant (ca 1529-1557)
The Attaingnant Dance Prints (1557)
Arr. Maggie Sansone
(c) 2009 Maggie's Music
From CD: A Celtic Fair

Index

Below are the tunes in alphabetical order.

23.	BARNEY BRALLAGHAN, melody and chords
24.	BARNEY BRALLAGHAN, arrangement
11.	BRETON AN DRO, F#m- 1st round
12.	BRETON AN DRO, Bm- 2nd and 3rd round
5.	BRETON JIG, melody and chords
6.	BRETON JIG, arrangement
21.	BUTTERFLY, melody and chords
22.	BUTTERFLY, arrangement
7.	CASTLEBAR, melody and chords
8.	CASTLEBAR, arrangement
13.	CIRCLE DANCE, melody and chords
14.	CIRCLE DANCE, arrangement
19.	COMB YOUR HAIR AND CURL IT, melody and chords
20.	COMB YOUR HAIR AND CURL IT, arrangement
33.	DONEGAL HIGHLAND, melody, back up arrangement
34.	DONEGAL HIGHLAND, arrangement
38.	FRENCH RENAISSANCE DANCES, melody and chords
39.	FRENCH RENAISSANCE DANCES, 2-part arrangements
17.	HIGH REEL, melody and chords
27.	HIGHLAND BOAT SONG, arrangement with alternate chords
28.	HIGHLAND BOAT SONG, arrangement with variation
37.	MAIDEN LANE, G and A, melody and chords
35.	MOTHER AND CHILD, melody and chords
29.	ROUND OF LOUDEAC, melody and chords in 2 octaves
30.	ROUND OF LOUDEAC, arrangement
1.	SCOTTISH BRANSLE, Intro
2.	SCOTTISH BRANSLE, Gm, melody and chords
3.	SCOTTISH BRANSLE, Gm, in 4 parts
4.	SCOTTISH BRANSLE, Am, in 4 parts
18.	SILVER SPEAR, melody and chords
31.	THE WREN, melody and chords
32.	THE WREN, 2 page arrangement
9.	TRAIN TO DUBLIN, melody and chords
10.	TRAIN TO DULBIN, arrangement
25.	VARIATION on PRETTY GIRL MIKLING A COW, melody and chords
26.	VARIATION on PRETTY GIRL MILKING A COW, 3 page arrangement
15.	WATCHMAKER, melody and chords in 2 octaves
16.	WATCHMAKER, arrangement
36.	WOMAN OF THE HOUSE, melody and chords